Congressional
Research Service
Informing the legislative debate since 1914 _____

The Federal Food Safety System: A Primer

Renée Johnson
Specialist in Agricultural Policy

September 2, 2014

Congressional Research Service

7-5700

www.crs.gov

RS22600

Summary

Numerous federal, state, and local agencies share responsibilities for regulating the safety of the U.S. food supply. Federal responsibility for food safety rests primarily with the Food and Drug Administration (FDA) and the U.S. Department of Agriculture (USDA). FDA, an agency of the Department of Health and Human Services, is responsible for ensuring the safety of all domestic and imported food products (except for most meats and poultry). FDA also has oversight of all seafood, fish, and shellfish products. USDA's Food Safety and Inspection Service (FSIS) regulates most meat and poultry and some egg products. State and local food safety authorities collaborate with federal agencies for inspection and other food safety functions, and they regulate retail food establishments. Other federal agencies also play a role. The Government Accountability Office (GAO) has identified as many as 15 federal agencies, including FDA and FSIS, as collectively administering at least 30 laws related to food safety. State and local food safety authorities collaborate with federal agencies for inspection and other food safety functions, and they regulate retail food establishments.

The combined efforts of the food industry and government regulatory agencies often are credited with making the U.S. food supply among the safest in the world. However, critics view this system as lacking the organization, regulatory tools, and resources to adequately combat foodborne illness—as evidenced by a series of widely publicized food safety problems, including concerns about adulterated food and food ingredient imports, and illnesses linked to various types of fresh produce, to peanut products, and to some meat and poultry products. Some critics also note that the organizational complexity of the U.S. food safety system as well as trends in U.S. food markets—for example, increasing imports as a share of U.S. food consumptions and increasing consumption of fresh, often unprocessed, foods—pose ongoing challenges to ensuring food safety.

Over the years, GAO has published a series of reports highlighting how food safety oversight in the United States is fragmented, and recommending broad restructuring of the nation's food safety system. Similar observations are noted in a series of food safety studies by the National Research Council (NRC) and Institute of Medicine (IOM), recommending that the core federal food safety responsibilities should reside within a single entity/agency, and have a unified administrative structure, clear mandate, and dedicated budget, and maintain full responsibility for oversight of the entire U.S. food supply.

The 111th Congress passed comprehensive food safety legislation with the FDA Food Safety Modernization Act (FSMA, P.L. 111-353). FSMA is the largest expansion of FDA's food safety authorities since the 1930s. Although numerous agencies share responsibility for regulating food safety, FSMA focused on foods regulated by FDA and amended FDA's existing structure and authorities, and did not directly address meat and poultry products under USDA's jurisdiction. Beyond these changes, some in Congress continue to push for additional policy reforms to address other perceived concerns about the safety of the U.S. food supply.

Contents

Figures

Tables

Appendixes

Contacts

Background

Americans spend more than $1 trillion on food each year, nearly half of it in restaurants, schools, and other places outside the home.[1] Federal laws give food manufacturers, distributors, and retailers the basic responsibility for assuring that foods are wholesome, safe, and handled under sanitary conditions. A number of federal agencies, cooperating with state, local, and international entities, play a major role in regulating food quality and safety under these laws.

The combined efforts of the food industry and the regulatory agencies often are credited with making the U.S. food supply among the safest in the world. Nonetheless, the Centers for Disease Control and Prevention (CDC) reports that each year an estimated one in six Americans—a total of 48 million people—becomes sick from contaminated food foodborne illnesses caused by contamination from any one of a number of microbial pathogens.[2] Of these, an estimated 128,000 cases require hospitalization and 3,000 cases result in death. In addition, experts have cited numerous other hazards to health, including the use of unapproved veterinary drugs, pesticides, and other dangerous substances in food commodities, of particular concern at a time when a growing share of the U.S. food supply is from overseas sources. These concerns, combined with the ongoing recurrence of major food safety-related incidents, have heightened public and media scrutiny of the U.S. food safety system and magnified congressional interest in the issue.

The Agencies and Their Roles

Numerous federal, state, and local agencies share responsibilities for regulating the safety of the U.S. food supply. Federal responsibility for food safety rests primarily with the Food and Drug Administration (FDA), which is part of the U.S. Department of Health and Human Services (HHS), and the Food Safety and Inspection Service (FSIS), which is part of the U.S. Department of Agriculture (USDA). FDA is responsible for ensuring that all domestic and imported food products—except for most meats and poultry—are safe, nutritious, wholesome, and accurately labeled. FDA also has oversight of all seafood, fish, and shellfish products. USDA's Food Safety and Inspection Service (FSIS) regulates most meat and poultry and some egg and fish products.

The Government Accountability Office (GAO) has identified as many as 15 federal agencies, including FDA and FSIS, as collectively administering at least 30 laws related to food safety.[3] **Appendix A** and **Appendix B** provide a brief comparative look at each of these agencies and their responsibilities. State and local food safety authorities collaborate with federal agencies for inspection and other food safety functions, and they regulate retail food establishments. This organizational complexity, and trends in U.S. food markets—for example, increasing imports as a share of U.S. food consumption and increasing consumption of fresh, often unprocessed, foods— pose ongoing challenges to ensuring food safety.

The text box below provides a comparison of FDA and USDA and other federal agencies' responsibilities for food safety and related food quality and other requirements.

---

[1] USDA, Economic Research Service (ERS) food sales data.

[2] U.S. Department of Health and Human Services, Centers for Disease Control and Prevention, "Estimates of Foodborne Illness in the United States," February 2011.

[3] GAO, *Federal Food Safety Oversight*, GAO-11-289, March 2011.

Comparison of Selected Agency Responsibilities for Food Safety and Quality

Agency	Responsibility
Food and Drug Administration (FDA)	• Food (but not meat)
	• Dietary supplements
	• Bottled water
	• Seafood
	• Wild game ("exotic" meat)
	• Eggs in the shell
U.S. Department of Agriculture (USDA)	• Grading of raw fruit and vegetables
	• Meat and Poultry
	• Eggs, processing and grading
	• Certifying organic production
National Oceanic and Atmospheric Administration	• Grading of fish and seafood
Environmental Protection Agency (EPA)	• Drinking water
	• Pesticide residues
Customs and Border Protection (CBP)	• Front-line enforcement and referral
Department of Justice (DOJ)	• Law enforcement
Federal Trade Commission (FTC)	• Advertising
Alcohol and Tobacco Tax and Trade Bureau (TTB)	• Alcohol

Source: CRS, as adapted by N. D. Fortin, *Introduction to Food Regulation in the United States*, Part 1, May 2008.

The division of food safety responsibility between FDA and USDA is rooted in the early history of U.S. food regulation. Congress created separate statutory frameworks when it enacted, in 1906, both the Pure Food and Drugs Act and the Meat Inspection Act. The former addressed the widespread marketing of intentionally adulterated foods, and its implementation was assigned to USDA's Bureau of Chemistry. The latter law addressed unsafe and unsanitary conditions in meat packing plants, and implementation was assigned to the USDA's Bureau of Animal Industry. This bifurcated system has been perpetuated and split further into additional food safety activities under additional agencies (for example, the Environmental Protection Agency, the National Marine Fisheries Service, and others) by a succession of statutes and executive directives. The separation of the two major food safety agencies was further reinforced when, in 1940, the President moved responsibilities for safe foods and drugs, other than meat and poultry, from USDA to the progenitor of HHS, the Federal Security Agency. Meat inspection remained in USDA. There has been discussion over time regarding whether this dispersal of food safety responsibilities has been problematic, or whether a reorganization would divert time and attention from other fundamental problems in the system.[4] **Figure 1** shows this history by providing a timeline of selected important dates for food safety in the United States.

---

[4] For a discussion of the history of federal food safety organization and of efforts to change it, see R.A. Merrill and J.K. Francer, "Organizing Federal Food Safety Regulation," *Seton Hall Law Review*, vol. 31:61, 2000. See also National Research Council, *Ensuring Safe Food from Production to Consumption*, National Academy Press, 1998.

Figure 1. Selected Important Dates for Food Safety in the United States, 1862-2011

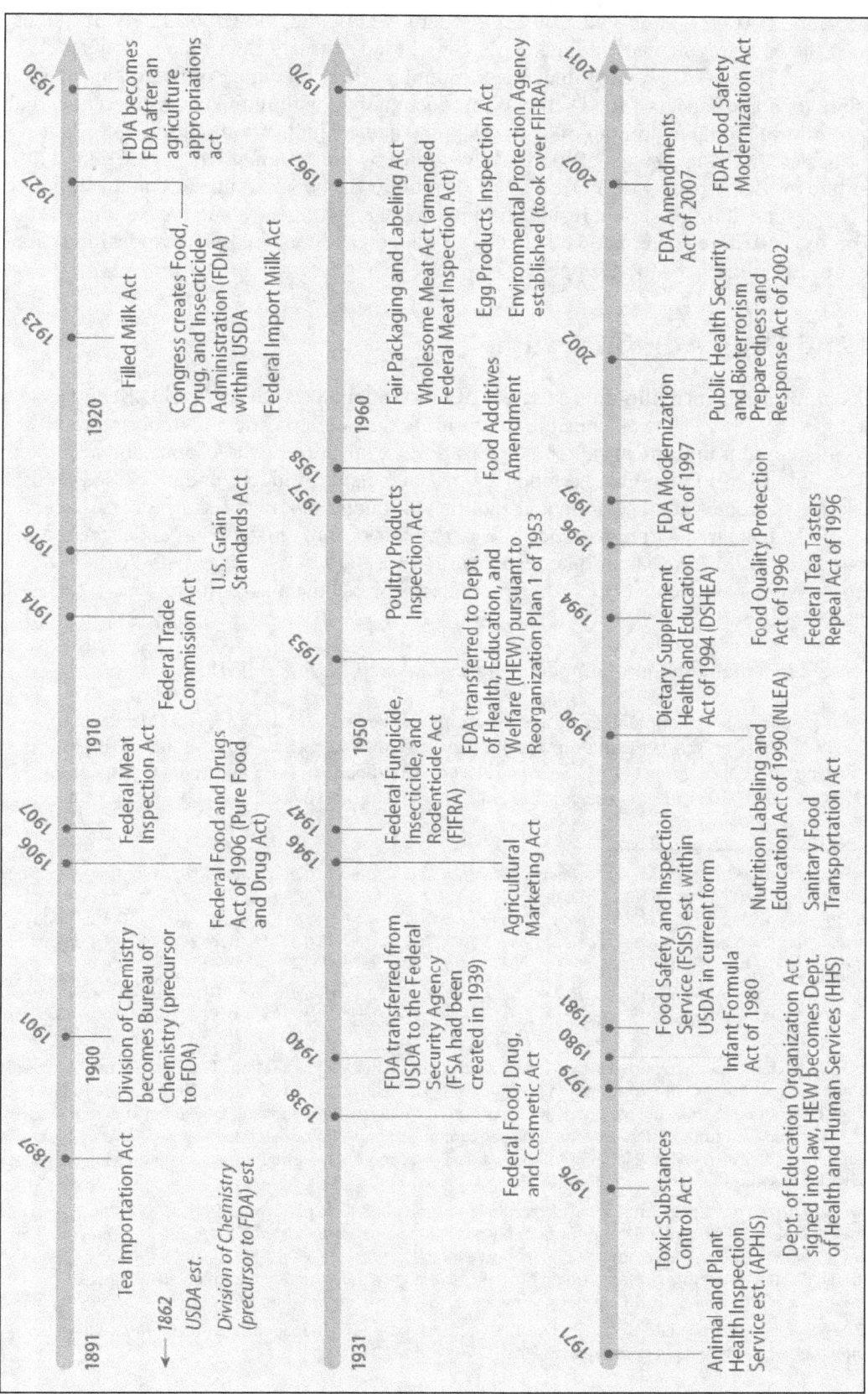

Source: Compiled by CRS from various government and industry sources (see footnote 4).

Over the years, GAO has published a series of reports highlighting how food safety oversight in the United States is fragmented, and recommending broad restructuring of the nation's food safety system.[5] These GAO reports document examples where a number of federal agencies are responsible for some aspect of food safety or product quality, with limited coordination and also sharing of information, resulting in often overlapping and/or duplication of efforts. Similar observations are noted in a series of food safety studies by the National Research Council (NRC) and Institute of Medicine (IOM).[6] The NRC/IOM studies further recommend that the core federal food safety responsibilities should reside within a single entity/agency, and have a unified administrative structure, clear mandate, dedicated budget, and maintain full responsibility for oversight of the entire U.S. food supply.

Food and Drug Administration

FDA has primary responsibility for the safety of most (about 80%-90%) of all U.S. domestic and imported foods.[7] The FDA is responsible for ensuring that all domestic and imported food products—except for most meats and poultry—are safe, nutritious, wholesome, and accurately labeled. Examples of FDA-regulated foods are produce, dairy products, and processed foods. FDA also has oversight of all seafood and shellfish products, and most fish products (except for catfish).[8] FDA has jurisdiction over meats from animals or birds that are not under the regulatory jurisdiction of FSIS. FDA shares some responsibility for the safety of eggs with FSIS. FDA has jurisdiction over establishments that sell or serve eggs or use them as an ingredient in their products.

As described in a memorandum of understanding between FDA and FSIS:[9]

> FDA is responsible for implementing and enforcing the Federal Food, Drug, and Cosmetic Act (21 U.S.C. 301, *et seq.*), the Public Health Service Act (42 U.S.C. 201, *et seq.*), the Fair Packaging and Labeling Act (15 U.S.C. 1451 *et seq.*), and parts of the Egg Products Inspection Act [21 U.S.C. §§1031 *et seq.*]. In carrying out its responsibilities under these acts, FDA conducts

---

[5] See, for example, GAO, *Opportunities to Reduce Potential Duplication in Government Programs, Save Tax Dollars, and Enhance Revenue* (GAO-11-318SP, March 2011); GAO, *Federal Food Safety and Security System: Fundamental Restructuring Is Needed to Address Fragmentation and Overlap,* GAO-04-588T, March 2004; and GAO, *Food Safety and Security: Fundamental Changes Needed to Ensure Safe Food,* GAO-02-47T, October 2001; GAO's reports on Federal Food Safety Oversight (2011, 2008 and 2005).

[6] NRC/IOM, *Enhancing Food Safety: The Role of the Food and Drug Administration,* 2010 (National Academy of Sciences); NRC/IOM, *Ensuring Safe Food from Production to Consumption,* 1998; and NRC/IOM, *Scientific Criteria for Safe Food,* 2003.

[7] Estimated by backing out the reported 10%-20% of foods under USDA's jurisdiction. The 20% estimate is based on information reported by GAO in "Revamping Oversight of Food Safety," prepared for the 2009 Congressional and Presidential Transition, and appears to represent proportions of total spending for food consumed at home. The 10% estimate is based on data from USDA-ERS on U.S. per capita food consumption at http://www.ers.usda.gov/data/foodconsumption/. See also DHS, "National Infrastructure Protection Plan: Agriculture and Food Sector Snapshot," http://www.dhs.gov/food-and-agriculture-sector.

[8] FSIS was authorized to inspect farmed catfish products under a 2008 farm bill provision (P.L. 110-246, §11016). The 2014 farm bill (P.L. 113-79, §12106) reconfirmed this provision and also mandated USDA and FDA enter into an agreement to improve interagency cooperation and prevent duplication; see MOU 225-14-0009 (between USDA's FSIS and FDA), http://www.fda.gov/aboutfda/partnershipscollaborations/memorandaofunderstandingmous/domesticmous/ucm396294 htm. FSIS has not yet implemented the catfish program.

[9] MOU 225-99-2001 (between USDA's FSIS and FDA), http://www.fda.gov/aboutfda/partnershipscollaborations/memorandaofunderstandingmous/domesticmous/ucm117094 htm.

---

inspections of establishments that manufacture, process, pack, or hold foods, with the exception of certain establishments that are regulated exclusively by FSIS. FDA also inspects vehicles and other conveyances, such as boats, trains, and airplanes, in which foods are transported or held in interstate commerce.

In addition, the 111th Congress passed comprehensive food safety legislation with the FDA Food Safety Modernization Act (FSMA, P.L. 111-353), amending FFDCA. FSMA was the largest expansion of FDA's food safety authorities since the 1930s.[10] FSMA did not directly address meat and poultry products under USDA's jurisdiction. New rules governing FDA's food inspection regime of both domestic and imported foods under the agency's jurisdiction are currently being developed and under public review and comment. For up-to-date information on FDA's ongoing rulemaking progress under FSMA, see FDA's website.[11]

In the Washington, DC, area, two FDA offices are the focal point for food safety-related activities. The Center for Food Safety and Applied Nutrition (CFSAN) is responsible for (1) conducting and supporting food safety research; (2) developing and overseeing enforcement of food safety and quality regulations; (3) coordinating and evaluating FDA's food surveillance and compliance programs; (4) coordinating and evaluating cooperating states' food safety activities; and (5) developing and disseminating food safety and regulatory information to consumers and industry. FDA's Center for Veterinary Medicine (CVM) is responsible for ensuring that all animal drugs, feeds (including pet foods), and veterinary devices are safe for animals, are properly labeled, and produce no human health hazards when used in food-producing animals.

The FDA also cooperates with over 400 state agencies across the nation to carry out a wide range of food safety regulatory activities. However, the state agencies are primarily responsible for actual inspection. FDA works with the states to set the safety standards for food establishments and commodities and evaluates the states' performance in upholding such standards as well as any federal standards that may apply. FDA also contracts with states to use their food safety agency personnel to carry out certain field inspections in support of FDA's own statutory responsibilities.

Food Safety and Inspection Service

FSIS regulates the safety, wholesomeness, and proper labeling of most domestic and imported meat and poultry and their products sold for human consumption, comprising roughly 10%-20% of the U.S. food supply.[12] As described in a memorandum of understanding between FDA and FSIS, FSIS's jurisdiction is as follows:[13]

> FSIS is responsible for implementing and enforcing the Federal Meat Inspection Act (21 U.S.C. 601, *et seq.*), the Poultry Products Inspection Act (21 U.S.C. 451, *et seq.*), and parts of the Egg Products Inspection Act (21 U.S.C. 1031, *et seq.*). In carrying out its responsibilities under these

---

[10] For more information, see CRS Report R40443, *The FDA Food Safety Modernization Act (P.L. 111-353)*. FSMA does not directly address meat and poultry products under USDA's jurisdiction.

[11] FDA, "The Law, Rules, and Guidance," http://www.fda.gov/Food/GuidanceRegulation/FSMA/ucm359436.htm. Selected summary information is provided in CRS Report R42885, *Food Safety Issues for the 113th Congress*.

[12] See footnote 7.

[13] MOU 225-99-2001 (between USDA's FSIS and FDA), http://www.fda.gov/aboutfda/partnershipscollaborations/memorandaofunderstandingmous/domesticmous/ucm117094.htm.

acts, FSIS places inspectors in meat and poultry slaughterhouses and in meat, poultry, and egg processing plants. FSIS also conducts inspections of warehouses, transporters, retail stores, restaurants, and other places where meat, poultry, and egg products are handled and stored. In addition, FSIS conducts voluntary inspections under the Agriculture Marketing Act (7 U.S.C. 1621, *et seq.*).

The Federal Meat Inspection Act (FMIA) of 1906, as amended, requires USDA to inspect all cattle, sheep, swine, goats, horses, mules, and other equines slaughtered and processed for human consumption. The Poultry Products Inspection Act (PPIA) of 1957, as amended, gives USDA the authority to inspect poultry meat. The PPIA mandates USDA inspection of any domesticated birds (chickens, turkeys, ducks, geese, guineas, ratites (ostrich, emu, and rhea), and squab (pigeons up to one month old)) intended for use as human food. The Egg Products Inspection Act, as amended, provides USDA authority to inspect liquid, frozen, and dried egg products. Each of these laws also contains provisions governing USDA's authority to label food products under its jurisdiction.[14]

Under the authority of the Agricultural Marketing Act of 1946 as amended, USDA's FSIS may provide voluntary inspection for buffalo, antelope, reindeer, elk, migratory waterfowl, game birds, and rabbits. This type of inspection is performed by FSIS on a fee-for-service basis. However, these meat and poultry species are still within the purview of FDA under FFDCA, whether or not inspected under the voluntary FSIS program. FDA has jurisdiction over meat products from such species in interstate commerce, even if they bear the USDA inspection mark. FDA also has jurisdiction over shell eggs. In addition, the 2008 farm bill requires that FSIS inspect and grade farmed catfish products.[15]

Meat and poultry animals and products undergo continuous (i.e., 100%) inspection, which may in turn act as a deterrent to fraud in some cases. FSIS inspects all meat and poultry animals to look for signs of disease, contamination, and other abnormal conditions, both before and after slaughter ("antemortem" and "postmortem," respectively), on a continuous basis—meaning that no animal may be slaughtered and dressed unless an inspector has examined it. One or more federal inspectors are on the line during all hours the plant is operating. Processing plants visited once every day by an FSIS inspector are considered to be under continuous inspection in keeping with the laws. Inspectors monitor operations, check sanitary conditions, examine ingredient levels and packaging, review records, verify food safety plans[16], and conduct statistical sampling and testing of products for pathogens and residues during their inspections.[17]

FSIS is responsible for certifying that foreign meat and poultry plants are operating under an inspection system equivalent to the U.S. system before they can export their product to the United States.[18] Meat and poultry imports are 100% visually inspected (process-based, documentation, labeling), although physical inspections of imports may be more random. FSIS conducts

---

[14] "A Guide to federal Food Labeling Requirements for meat, Poultry, and Egg Products," prepared for USDA Food Safety and Inspection Service by Hogan & Hartson, LLP, August, 2007.

[15] P.L. 110-246, §11016 (Inspection and Grading). USDA has not yet finished its catfish inspection rule (76 *Federal Register* 10434, February 24, 2011), and will inspect catfish facilities when the rule is finalized.

[16] In a Hazard Analysis and Critical Control Point (HACCP) plan a facility must identify each point in its processes where contamination could occur ("critical control point") and have a plan to control it, as well as document and maintain records.

[17] For more information, see CRS Report RL32922, *Meat and Poultry Inspection: Background and Selected Issues*.

[18] For information, see FSIS, "FSIS Import Procedures for Meat, Poultry & Egg Products," http://www.fsis.usda.gov/.

evaluations of foreign meat safety programs and visits establishments to determine whether they are providing a level of safety equivalent to that of U.S. safeguards. No foreign plant can ship meat or poultry to the United States unless its country has received such an FSIS determination.

Twenty-seven states operate their own meat and/or poultry inspection programs. FSIS is statutorily responsible for ensuring that the states' programs are at least equal to the federal program.[19] Plants processing meat and poultry under state inspection can market their products only within the state. If a state chooses to discontinue its own inspection program, or if FSIS determines that it does not meet the agency's equivalency standards, FSIS must assume the responsibility for inspection if the formerly state-inspected plants are to remain in operation. FSIS also has cooperative agreements with more than two dozen states under which state inspection personnel are authorized to carry out federal inspection in meat and/or poultry plants. Products from these plants may travel in interstate commerce.[20]

Centers for Disease Control and Prevention

CDC is responsible for (1) monitoring, identifying, and investigating foodborne disease problems to determine the contributing factors; (2) working with FDA, FSIS, NMFS, state and local public health departments, universities, and industry to develop control methods; and (3) evaluating the effect of control methods. CDC's "FoodNet" is a collaborative project with the FDA and USDA to improve data collection on foodborne illness outbreaks. FoodNet includes active surveillance of clinical microbiology laboratories to obtain a more accurate accounting of positive test results for foodborne illness; a physician survey to determine testing and laboratory practices; population surveys to identify illnesses not reported to doctors; and research studies to obtain new and more precise information about which food items or other exposures may cause diseases. FoodNet data allow CDC to have a clearer picture of the incidence and causes of foodborne illness and to establish baseline data against which to measure the success of changes in food safety programs. The Public Health Service Act (42 U.S.C. §§201, *et seq.*) provides legislative authority for CDC's food safety-related activities.

National Marine Fisheries Service

Although the FDA is the primary agency responsible for ensuring the safety, wholesomeness, and proper labeling of domestic and imported seafood products, the National Marine Fisheries Service (NMFS), which is part of the U.S. Department of Commerce, conducts, on a fee-for-service basis, a voluntary seafood inspection and grading program that focuses on marketing and quality attributes of U.S. fish and shellfish.[21] The primary legislative authority for NMFS's inspection program is the Agricultural Marketing Act of 1946, as amended (7 U.S.C. §§1621 *et seq.*). NMFS has approximately 160 seafood safety and quality inspectors, and inspection services are funded with user fees. NMFS works with FDA, which helps provide training and

---

[19] USDA, "Listing of Participating States," http://www.fsis.usda.gov/regulations_&_policies/ Listing_of_participating_states/index.asp.

[20] The 2008 farm bill (P.L. 110-246, §11017) contained new provisions intended to enable more interstate shipment of state-inspected products.

[21] NOAA Seafood Inspection Program, http://www.seafood.nmfs.noaa.gov/Program_Services.html. See also CRS Report RS22797, *Seafood Safety: Background and Issues.*

other technical assistance to NMFS. Under the program, NMFS inspects a reported 20% of the seafood consumed in the United States.[22]

Environmental Protection Agency

EPA has the statutory responsibility for ensuring that the chemicals used on food crops do not endanger public health. EPA's Office of Pesticide Programs is the part of the agency that (1) registers new pesticides and determines residue levels for regulatory purposes; (2) performs special reviews of pesticides of concern; (3) reviews and evaluates all the health data on pesticides; (4) reviews data on pesticides' effects on the environment and on other species; (5) analyzes the costs and benefits of pesticide use; and (6) interacts with EPA regional offices, state regulatory counterparts, other federal agencies involved in food safety, the public, and others to keep them informed of EPA regulatory actions. The Federal Insecticide, Fungicide, and Rodenticide Act, as amended (7 U.S.C. §§136 *et seq.*), and the Federal Food, Drug, and Cosmetic Act, as amended (21 U.S.C. §§301 *et seq.*), are the primary authorities for EPA's activities in this area.

Agricultural Marketing Service

USDA's Agricultural Marketing Service (AMS) is responsible for establishing quality and marketing grades and standards for many foods (including dairy products, fruits and vegetables, livestock, meat, poultry, seafoods, and shell eggs), and for certifying quality programs and conducting quality grading services. Accordingly, AMS is primarily responsible for ensuring product *quality* and not food *safety*. USDA programs establishing quality grade standards to encourage uniformity and consistency in commercial practices are provided for under the Agricultural Marketing Act of 1946 (7 U.S.C. §1621).

AMS also administers the Pesticide Data Program (PDP), a cooperative federal-state residue testing program through which it collects data on residual pesticides, herbicides, insecticides, fungicides, and growth regulators in over 50 different commodities.[23] The pesticides and commodities to be tested each year are chosen based on EPA data needs, and on information about the types and amounts foods consumed, in particular, by infants and children. Authorization for the program is under the Federal Food, Drug, and Cosmetic Act, as amended by the 1996 Food Quality Protection Act (21 U.S.C. §§301 *et seq.*).

Other Federal Agencies

Among the other agencies that play a role in food safety, USDA's Agricultural Research Service (ARS) performs food safety research in support of FSIS's inspection program. It has scientists working in animal disease bio-containment laboratories in Plum Island, NY, and Ames, IA. USDA's Animal and Plant Health Inspection Service (APHIS) indirectly protects the nation's food supply through programs to protect plant and animal resources from domestic and foreign pests and diseases, such as brucellosis and bovine spongiform encephalopathy (BSE, or "mad

---

[22] NOAA, "Inspecting Seafood—A Highly Trained Nose Knows," *Fishwatch.gov*, October 2012.

[23] For more information, see AMS's website, http://www.ams.usda.gov/AMSv1.0/pdp.

cow" disease). The Department of Homeland Security (DHS) is to coordinate many food security activities, including at U.S. borders.

Congressional Committees

In the Senate, food safety issues are considered by the Committees on Agriculture, Nutrition, and Forestry; Homeland Security and Governmental Affairs; and Health, Education, Labor, and Pensions. In the House, various food safety activities fall under the jurisdiction of the Committees on Agriculture; Energy and Commerce; Oversight and Government Reform; and Science. Agriculture subcommittees of the House and Senate Appropriations Committees also serve oversight and funding roles in how the major agencies carry out food safety policies.

Funding for Federal Food Safety Programs

Historically, federal funding and staffing levels between FDA and FSIS have been disproportionate to their respective responsibilities for addressing food safety activities. Although FSIS is responsible for roughly 10%-20% of the U.S. food supply, it has received about 60% of the two agencies' combined food safety budget. Although FDA has been responsible for 80%-90% of the U.S. food supply, a few years ago it received about 40% of the combined budget for federal food safety activities (**Table 1**). Staffing levels also have varied considerably among the two agencies: FSIS staff numbered around 9,400 FTEs in FY2010, while FDA staff working on food-related activities numbers about 3,400 FTEs.

In recent years, however, the balance of overall funding for food safety between FDA and USDA has started to shift. Congressional appropriators have increased funding for FDA food activities, which more than doubled from $435.5 million in FY2005 to $882.8 million in FY2014 (**Table 1**). Funding for FSIS remained mostly unchanged to slightly lower overall. The Food Safety Modernization Act (FSMA) also provided for additional limited funding through certain types of industry-paid user fees.

FSMA—comprehensive food safety legislation enacted in the 111th Congress—authorized additional appropriations and staff for FDA's future food safety activities.[24] FSMA was the largest expansion of FDA's food safety authorities since the 1930s. Among its many provisions, FSMA authorized increased frequency of inspections at food facilities, tightened record-keeping requirements, extended oversight to certain farms, and also mandated product recalls. It required food processing, manufacturing, shipping, and other facilities to conduct a food safety plan of the most likely safety hazards, and design and implement risk-based controls. It also mandated improvements to the nation's foodborne illness surveillance systems and increased scrutiny of food imports, among other provisions. FSMA did not directly address meat and poultry products under USDA's jurisdiction.

Although Congress authorized appropriations when it enacted FSMA, it did not provide the funding needed for FDA to perform these activities. After FSMA was signed into law in January 2011, concerns were voiced about whether there would be enough money to overhaul the U.S. food safety system and also whether expanded investment in this area was appropriate in the

---

[24] P.L. 111-353 amended the Federal Food, Drug, and Cosmetic Act (FFDCA).

current budgetary climate.[25] Prior to enactment, the Congressional Budget Office (CBO) estimated that implementing FSMA could increase net federal spending subject to appropriation by about $1.4 billion over a five-year period (FY2011-FY2015).[26] This cost estimate covers activities at FDA and other federal agencies, and does not include offsetting revenue from the collection of new user fees authorized under FSMA.[27] FSMA did not impose any new facility registration fees. Prior to enactment, CBO estimated that about $240 million in new fees would be collected over the five-year period (FY2011-FY2015), with "insignificant" collections from possible revenue and direct spending increases from new criminal penalties.[28] Taking into account these new fees, CBO estimated that covering the five-year cost of new requirements within FDA, including more frequent inspections, would require additional outlays of $1.1 billion.

FDA continues to implement regulations under FSMA. Although Congress has added to FDA's budget for its Foods Program in the past few years, agency officials claim that FDA will need an additional $400 million to $450 million more per year above its FY2012 base to fully implement FSMA.[29]

Funding levels specific to food safety responsibilities at other federal and state agencies are not readily available.

FDA staff working on food-related activities also has increased. Among its many provisions, FSMA mandated an increase in the number of food safety inspectors within FDA and expanded the agency's authority to increase inspection of domestic and foreign food facilities. FSMA states a "goal of not fewer than ... 5,000 staff members in fiscal year 2014."[30] Instead, FDA reports actual staffing levels at 3,800 FTEs in FY2014 (**Table 1**). FSIS staff number between 9,300 and 9,400 FTEs, depending on the year.

The discrepancy between the number of FDA and FSIS inspectors is, in part, attributable to differences in how each agency fulfills its respective inspection mandate. Whereas FDA inspection involves primarily review and sampling, FSIS personnel inspect all meat and poultry animals at slaughter on a continuous basis, requiring that at least one federal inspector is on the line during all hours the plant is operating. Processing inspection does not require an FSIS inspector to remain constantly on the production line or to inspect every item. Instead, inspectors are on site daily to monitor the plant's adherence to the standards for sanitary conditions, ingredient levels, and packaging, and to conduct statistical sampling and testing of products. Because all plants are visited daily, processing inspection also is considered to be continuous.

---

[25] See "Food Safety Bill Advocates Expect Funding Fight," *Food Safety News*, January 4, 2011.

[26] CBO, Cost Estimate, "S. 510, Food Safety Modernization Act, as reported by the Senate Committee on Health, Education, Labor, and Pensions on December 18, 2009, incorporating a manager's amendment released on August 12, 2010," August 12, 2010, http://www.cbo.gov/ftpdocs/117xx/doc11794/s510.pdf; reflects the Senate amendment to S. 510. Estimated total costs would be covered by a combination of user fees and direct appropriations (budget authority).

[27] FSMA authorized additional appropriations and staff for FDA's future food safety activities and authorized new user fees. New fees authorized under FSMA include an annual fee for participants in the voluntary qualified importer program (VQIP) and three fees for certain periodic activities involving reinspection, recall, and export certification. FSMA, P.L. 111-353, §§107 and 401. Details of these annual and periodic fees are presented in CRS Report R40443, *The FDA Food Safety Modernization Act (P.L. 111-353)*.

[28] As estimated by CBO, these fees would be phased in as follows: $15 million (FY2011), $27 million (FY2012); $47 million (FY2013); $63 million (FY2014); and $89 million (FY2015).

[29] FDA, *Building Domestic Capacity to Implement the FDA Food Safety Modernization Act (FSMA)*, May 2013.

[30] FSMA, P.L. 111-353, §401. By fiscal year, staff level increases were authorized to a total of not fewer than: 4,000 staff members (FY2011); 4,200 staff (FY2012); 4,600 staff (FY2013); and 5,000 staff (FY2014).

Table 1. Food Safety Appropriations

(FTEs as indicated, and budget and appropriation figures in millions of dollars)

Agency/Year	FTEs[a]	Appropriation[b]	Program Level, Including Fees[c]
HHS Food and Drug Administration (FDA), "Foods" Subtotal			
FY2009 Actual	2,995	712.8	712.8
FY2010 Actual	3,387	783.2	783.2
FY2011 Actual	3,605	836.2	836.2
FY2012 Actual	3,546	866.1	882.7
FY2013 Operating Plan (post-sequestration)	3,626	796.6[d]	813.2
FY2014, Appropriation (P.L. 113-76)	3,805	882.8	900.3
FY2015: Administration Request	4,236	903.4	1,124.3[e]
FY2015, H.R. 4800, as reported	NA	903.4	913.8
FY2015, S. 2389, as reported	NA	903.4	913.8
USDA Food Safety and Inspection Service (FSIS)			
FY2009 Actual	9,343	971.6	1,105.7
FY2010 Actual	9,401	1,018.5	1,172.4
FY2011 Actual	9,465	1,008.5	1,187.2
FY2012 Actual	9,351	1,004.4	1,169.1
FY2013 Operating Plan (post-sequestration)	9,158	977.3[f]	1,163.7
FY2014, Appropriation (P.L. 113-76)	9,360	1,010.7	1,183.2
FY2015: Administration Request	9,098	1,001.4	1,174.9
FY2015, H.R. 4800, as reported	NA	1,005.2	NA
FY2015, S. 2389, as reported	NA	1,022.8	NA

Sources: CRS, from H.R. 4800, S. 2389, FDA FY2013 Sequestration Operating Plan, FDA FY2014 Operating Plan, and annual agency budget justifications for FDA (http://www.fda.gov/AboutFDA/ReportsManualsForms/Reports/BudgetReports/default.htm) and FSIS (http://www.obpa.usda.gov/explan_notes.html). NA=not available.

Notes:

a.   Staffing in full time equivalents (FTEs).

b.   Does not include existing or proposed user fees or other 'non-federal' payments.

c.   Includes user fees. For FDA, reflects actual or planned fees through FY2014, and for FY2015. enacted, CR, and requested fee amounts. For FSIS, includes existing fees and trust fund for overtime, holiday, and voluntary inspection.

d.   FDA's "FY2013 Sequestration Operating Plan." and "FY2014 Operating Plan."

e.   The Administration's requested Foods program level total includes $10.4 million in authorized fees relating to food reinspection, food and feed recall, and the voluntary qualified importer program; and other proposed fees covering food facility registration and inspection, food import, international courier, and food contact notification fees. The "Appropriation" amount excludes fees (both authorized and proposed) from the requested "Program Level" amount.

f.   Reported by USDA for FSIS in its "Fiscal Year 2013 Operating Plan" and reflects "2013 Enacted w/ Sequester and Rescissions."

Federal Food Safety Inspections

As funding for FDA's food safety oversight and the number of inspection personnel has increased, so too has the number of food facilities subject to FDA inspection. Food facilities subject to FDA inspection has been increasing sharply in recent years, rising from about 59,000 in 2004 to nearly 76,000 in 2011 (**Table 2**). Of these, about one-fourth underwent FDA inspection.

Table 2. FDA Food-Related Inspection Data, FY2004-FY2012

	FY04	FY05	FY06	FY07	FY08	FY09	FY10	FY11	FY12
Employees[a]	3,082	2,943	2,774	2,569	2,614	2,995	3,387	3,605	3,757
Field FTEs	2,172	2,059	1,962	1,806	1,861	2,166	2,516	2,729	2,824
HQ FTEs	910	884	812	763	753	829	871	876	933
Inspections[b]	21,876	19,774	17,730	17,038	16,277	17,972	19,024	21,554	24,513
Domestic Facilities (FDA Inspection)[c]	59,305	61,930	62,929	65,520	67,819	66,196	73,930	75,990	NA
Inspections	17,032	15,773	14,547	14,339	14,966	16,087	17,640	19,141	NA
% Inspections	29%	25%	23%	22%	22%	24%	24%	25%	NA

Sources: Compiled by CRS from various sources or provided by FDA. NA=not available.

a. FDA Budget Explanatory Notes for Committee on Appropriations, various years (http://www.fda.gov/AboutFDA/ReportsManualsForms/Reports/BudgetReports/default.htm); and HHS OIG, *FDA Inspections of Domestic Food Facilities* (OEI-02-08-00080). FY2004-FY2010 employee data are actual numbers of program level FTEs (full-time equivalents) reported in FDA annual budget documents in "FDA Program Resources Table" for Foods, except that the FY2004 numbers are from the FY2006 annual Food and Drug Administration, *President's Budget Request*, "Narrative by Activity, Foods—Center for Food Safety and Applied Nutrition." FY2011-FY2012 data are from the FY2013 budget request.

b. FY2004-FY2010 inspection data are actual numbers of "Grand Total Food Establishment Inspections" (which include FDA and State Contract Inspections), from the FY2006-FY2012 annual Food and Drug Administration, *President's Budget Request*, Field Activities—Office of Regulatory Affairs (ORA), "Field Foods Program Activity Data." FY2011-FY2013 inspection data are from the FY2013 budget request. These data may differ with other data reported by FDA's Office of Inspector General (OIG) (see, for example, HHS, OIG, *Vulnerabilities in FDA's Oversight of State Food Facility Inspections* (OEI-02-09-00430), Table 1, December 2011, http://oig.hhs.gov/oei/reports/oei-02-09-00430.pdf).

c. Data are FDA Office of Legislation (September 22, 2010, and May 7, 2012, communication), and update information in FDA, "Annual Report HHS OIG, *FDA Inspections of Domestic Food Facilities* (OEI-02-08-00080), Table 1, April 2010.

In addition, since 2004, some 450,000 domestic and foreign food facilities are registered with the agency, and are potentially subject to inspection (**Table 3**). These data are drawn from a requirement set by Congress in 2002, following the enactment of the Public Health Security and Bioterrorism Preparedness and Response Act ("Bioterrorism Act", P.L. 107-188). The Bioterrorism Act requires that domestic and foreign facilities be registered with FDA and that FDA be given advance notice on shipments of imported food. Under the act, facilities that manufacture, process, pack, or hold food for human or animal consumption in the United States were required to register with FDA by December 12, 2003. Domestic facilities must register whether or not food from the facility enters interstate commerce. Foreign facilities that manufacture/process, pack, or hold food also must register unless food from that facility undergoes further processing (including packaging) by another foreign facility before the food is exported to the United States.[31] The total number of registered food facilities does not reflect the precise number of food facilities subject to FDA inspection, since these data include facilities under USDA's jurisdiction, among other facilities.

Table 3. Registered Food Facilities, FY2004-FY2012

	FY04	FY05	FY06	FY07	FY08	FY09	FY10	FY11	FY12
All Registered Food Facilities	214,253	253,006	288,092	323,590	356,287	391,281	418,593	438,305	449,859
Domestic	92,719	104,555	115,902	129,345	141,703	154,883	166,160	167,033	171,552
Foreign	121,534	148,451	172,190	194,245	214,584	236,398	252,433	271,272	278,307

Source: Compiled by CRS from data on registered domestic and foreign facilities under FFDCA §415 [21 U.S.C. §350d]; FDA's annual reporting requirements of these data are at FFDCA §1003 [21 U.S.C. §393]

Notes: Number of registrants as of November 18, 2013. Available FY2012 data are from FDA, "Registration Statistics," http://www.fda.gov/food/guidanceregulation/foodfacilityregistration/ucm236512.htm. FY2004-2011 data are FDA Office of Legislation (September 22, 2010, and May 7, 2012, communication); FDA, "Annual Report on Food Facilities, Food Imports, and FDA Foreign Offices" for 2011 and 2012,

Various estimates of unannounced compliance inspections of domestic establishments by FDA officials range from once every five years to once every 10 years, on average, although the agency claims to visit about 6,000 so-called high-risk facilities on an annual basis. FDA relies on notifications from within the industry or from other federal or state inspection personnel, as well as other sources, to alert it to situations calling for increased inspection. GAO reported that, in 2000, FDA inspections covered only about 1% of the food imported under its jurisdiction.[32] Changes to FDA's import regime now being implemented under FSMA are expected to address some of these concerns.

By comparison, the number of regulated meat and poultry facilities under USDA's jurisdiction is much lower, and has remained more stable over time (**Table 4**). During the past decade, USDA inspected an average of about 6,300 establishments each year, including Talmadge-Aiken plants. (In Talmadge-Aiken plants, state inspectors perform inspections, but are supervised by federal inspectors.) In 2012, USDA reported that it conducted inspections in 6,263 establishments.[33] This compares to 2002, when USDA reported that it conducted inspections in 6,000 establishments. The number of Talmadge-Aiken plants has increased to 343 facilities in 2012, from 235 in 2002.

About 1,100 of the establishments under FSIS's jurisdiction either slaughter, or slaughter and process, livestock or poultry.[34] More than 4,000 facilities only process meat and poultry, and about 80 process egg products. In addition to inspecting domestic meat, poultry, and egg establishments, FSIS also performs re-inspections of imported meat, poultry, and egg products at about 140 import re-inspection facilities.

---

[31] Owners, operators, or agents in charge of domestic or foreign facilities that manufacture/process, pack, or hold food for consumption in the United States are required to register the facility with the FDA. See FDA, "Registration of Food Facilities," http://www.fda.gov/Food/GuidanceComplianceRegulatoryInformation/RegistrationofFoodFacilities/default.htm.

[32] GAO, *Fundamental Changes Needed to Ensure Safe Food* (GAO-02-47T), October 10, 2001, http://www.gao.gov/new.items/d0247t.pdf.

[33] USDA, 2013 Explanatory Notes (FSIS), p. 21-1, http://www.obpa.usda.gov/21fsis2013notes.pdf.

[34] FSIS's inspection directory, http://www.fsis.usda.gov/wps/portal/fsis/topics/inspection/mpi-directory.

Of the roughly 9,200 FSIS staff, approximately 8,000 of them, including about 1,000 veterinarians, are in about 6,300 meat slaughtering and/or processing plants nationwide.

Table 4. FSIS Employees, Inspectors, and Establishments, FY2002-2012

	FY02	FY03	FY04	FY05	FY06	FY07	FY08	FY09	FY10	FY11	FY12
Employees	9,151	9,170	9,125	9,157	9,029	9,166	9,289	9,256	9,333	9,295	9,235
HQ	634	688	688	744	709	674	707	726	710	680	651
Field	8,517	8,482	8,437	8,413	8,320	8,492	8,582	8,530	8,623	8,615	8,584
Inspectors	7,600	7,560	7,587	7,583	7,865	7,800	7,566	7,540	7,563	7,556	NA
Establishments	6,300	6,400	6,300	6,250	6,282	6,200	6,200	6,286	6,278	6,290	6,263
Talmadge-Aiken	235	359	364	361	368	354	382	341	356	364	343

Source: USDA, Annual USDA Budget Explanatory Notes for Committee on Appropriations. Employees are permanent, full-time on September 30. FSIS also has part-time and temporary positions that have averaged nearly 500 employees in recent years.

Notes: A Talmadge-Aiken plant is a federal plant with state inspection program personnel operating under Federal supervisors. Much of the agency's work is conducted in cooperation with federal, state and municipal agencies, as well as private industry.

Appendix A. Major Federal Food Safety Agencies and Selected Laws

Agency	Major Responsibilities and Activities	Primary Authorities
Department of Health and Human Services		
Food and Drug Administration (FDA)[a]	Ensures that all domestic and imported foods, except processed egg products and major types of meat and poultry, are safe, wholesome, and properly labeled, by setting safety and sanitation standards, periodically inspecting manufacturing facilities, reviewing records of and spot-checking imports. Also oversees the safety of animal drugs and feeds, including those used in food-producing animals.	Federal Food, Drug, and Cosmetic Act (FFDCA; 21 U.S.C. §§301-399a) as amended; Public Health Service Act (42 U.S.C. §201), Egg Products Inspection Act (21 U.S.C. §1031); Federal Import Milk Act (21 U.S.C. §§141-149); Fair Packaging and Labeling Act (15 U.S.C. §§1451-1461); Federal Anti-Tampering Act (18 U.S.C. §1365); Pesticide Monitoring Improvements Act of 1988 (21 U.S.C. §1401)
Centers for Disease Control and Prevention (CDC)	Monitors, identifies, and investigates foodborne diseases; develops and evaluates improved epidemiological and laboratory methods.	Public Health Service Act (42 U.S.C. §201)
Department of Agriculture		
Food Safety Inspection Service (FSIS)[a]	Regulates the safety, wholesomeness and proper labeling of most commercial types of both domestic and imported meat and poultry, catfish products, and processed egg products, by approving establishment designs, safety plans; inspecting every animal and carcass in slaughtering plants and daily inspecting all meat and poultry processing plants; determining the equivalency of importing countries' meat and poultry safety systems.	Federal Meat Inspection Act (21 U.S.C. §§601-695); Poultry Products Inspection Act (21 U.S.C. §§451-472); Egg Products Inspection Act (21 U.S.C. §§1031-1056); Humane Methods of Slaughter Act of 1978 (7 U.S.C. §§1902, 1904, 21 U.S.C. §§603, 610, 620); Federal Anti-Tampering Act (18 U.S.C. §1365); Agricultural Marketing Act of 1946 (7 U.S.C. §1622); Richard B. Russell National School Lunch Act (42 U.S.C. §§1751-1770), as amended by Child Nutrition and WIC Reauthorization Acts (42 U.S.C. §1762a(h))
Animal and Plant Health Inspection Service (APHIS)	Oversees animal and plant health, including the prevention of foreign diseases and pests, and eradication and containment of such problems domestically (including those that threaten public health).	Animal Health Protection Act (7 U.S.C. §§8301-8322); Plant Health Protection Act (7 U.S.C. §§7701-7721); Agricultural Bioterrorism Act of 2002 (7 U.S.C. §8401)
Agricultural Marketing Service (AMS)	Establishes quality and marketing grades and standards for dairy products, fruits and vegetables, livestock, meat, poultry, seafoods, and shell eggs; certifies quality programs; conducts quality grading services, generally user fee-funded.	Agricultural Marketing Act of 1946 (7 U.S.C. §§1621-1638d), Perishable Agricultural Commodities Act, 1930 (7 U.S.C. §§499a- 499s); Federal Seed Act (7 U.S.C. §§1551-1611)
Food and Nutrition Service (FNS)	Encourages and coordinates efforts to ensure the safety of foods in school lunch and other domestic programs.	Program subsidies authorized by Richard B. Russell National School Lunch Act (42 U.S.C. §§1751-1770), as amended by Child Nutrition and WIC Reauthorization Acts (42 U.S.C. §1762a(h))
Grain Inspection, Packers and Stockyards Administration (GIPSA)	Sets quality standards for and tests grains and related commodities, primarily for marketing purposes.	U.S. Grain Standards Act (7 U.S.C. §§71-87k), Agricultural Marketing Act of 1946 (7 U.S.C. §§1622, 1624)

Agency	Major Responsibilities and Activities	Primary Authorities
Agricultural Research Service (ARS)	Conducts in-house USDA research on agricultural and food topics, of which food safety is one of many.	Numerous laws dating to the Department of Agriculture Organic Act of 1862 (7 U.S.C. §2201 note), up through and including recent omnibus farm laws
National Institute of Food and Agriculture (NIFA) (formerly Cooperative State Research, Education, and Extension Service)	Coordinates and administers federal funding of land grant and other institutions to conduct agricultural and food research, education and extension activities; food safety is one of many subject areas.	Numerous laws dating to the Department of Agriculture Organic Act of 1862, up through and including recent omnibus farm laws
Department of Commerce		
National Oceanic and Atmospheric Administration (NOAA)	Offers a variety of voluntary seafood safety and quality inspection services on a fee-for-service basis.	Agricultural Marketing Act of 1946 (7 U.S.C. §§1622, 1624); Lacey Act (16 U.S.C. §3371); Fish and Wildlife Act of 1956 (16 U.S.C. §742)
U.S. Environmental Protection Agency (EPA)	Regulates the use of certain chemicals and substances that present an unreasonable risk of injury to health or the environment. Regulates pesticide products; sets maximum allowable tolerances for residue levels on food commodities and animal feeds. Sets national drinking water standards and consults with FDA. Sets scientific water quality criteria for rivers, lakes, and streams that are protective of human health and wildlife.	Federal Food, Drug, and Cosmetic Act (21 U.S.C. §§301-399a), as amended; Federal Insecticide, Fungicide, and Rodenticide Act (7 U.S.C. §§136-136y), as amended by the Food Quality Protection Act of 1996 (21 U.S.C. §346a); Clean Water Act (33 U.S.C. 1251-1387); Safe Drinking Water Act of 1974 (21 U.S.C. §349 and 42 U.S.C. §§300f-300j-26); Toxic Substance Control Act (15 U.S.C. §§2601-2697)
Federal Trade Commission (FTC)	Enforces federal prohibitions against unfair or deceptive acts or practices in trade, including consumer deception regarding foods.	Federal Trade Commission Act (15 U.S.C. §§41-58)
Department of the Treasury		
Alcohol and Tobacco Tax and Trade Bureau (ATF)	Administers and enforces laws on the production, safety, distribution and use of alcoholic beverages.	Federal Alcohol Administration Act (27 U.S.C. §§201-219a); Internal Revenue Code (26 U.S.C. Ch. 51)
Department of Homeland Security		
U.S. Customs and Border Protection (CBP)	Coordinates many food security activities, including inspecting imports of food, plants, and animals at the border. Conducts agricultural border inspection activities formerly done by APHIS.	Homeland Security Act of 2002 (6 U.S.C. §101); Tariff Act of 1930 (19 U.S.C. §§1202-1654)

Source: Prepared by CRS based in part on various reports by the Government Accountability Office, including GAO, *Federal Food Safety Oversight*, GAO-11-289, March 2011. Does not include two USDA agencies included by GAO (Research, Education, and Economics (REE) agencies: National Economic Research Service (ERS) and National Agricultural Statistics Service (NASS).

a.   These agencies have the leading food safety regulatory authorities.

Appendix B. Selected Comparison of FSIS and FDA Responsibilities

Activity	Food Safety and Inspection Service	Food and Drug Administration (Foods Program only)
Primary Authorizations	Federal Meat Inspection Act (21 U.S.C. 601), Poultry Products Inspection Act (21 U.S.C. 451), Egg Products Inspection Act (21 U.S.C. 1031)	As may be amended by the FDA Food Safety Modernization Act (FSMA): Federal Food, Drug, and Cosmetic Act (FFDCA; 21 U.S.C. 301; Public Health Service Act (42 U.S.C. 201); Egg Products Inspection Act (21 U.S.C. 1031); Public Health Security and Bioterrorism Preparedness and Response Act (21 U.S.C. 341)
Foods Regulated	Major types of domestic and imported meat and poultry and their products; catfish products; processed (dried, frozen, liquid) egg products (20% of at-home U.S. food spending)	All other domestic and imported foods, also animal drugs and feeds including those used in food-producing animals (80% of at-home U.S. food spending)
Funding (FY2012)	Appropriated: $1.004 billion for FY2012. Expected user fees are estimated to include another $150 million. Including authorized fees, total available funding is estimated at about $1.154 billion.	Appropriated: $866.1 million for FDA's Foods Program, not including funding from expected user fees. Expected user fees are estimated to include another $16 million. Including authorized fees, total available funding is estimated at about $882.7 million.
Staff (2012)	9,400 FTEs	3,500 FTEs
Domestic facilities	6,300 slaughter and/or processing establishments	68,000 subject to inspection
Inspection Approach	Ante- and post-mortem inspection of every animal, carcass and part; traditionally organoleptic (but see "Food safety plans" below); only USDA-inspected and passed products may enter commerce	Prohibits adulteration or misbranding; relies on facilities that manufacture, process, pack, or hold food for humans or animals to meet prescribed standards (e.g., regarding additives, contaminants, etc.); all facilities must register, report changes in timely manner.
Required inspection frequency	Slaughter plants: all times of operation; processing plants: at least once daily	FSMA requires increased inspection rates for any registered facility, particularly those identified as "high-risk." Domestic high-risk facilities are to be inspected not less than once in the five-year period after enactment, and not less than once every three years thereafter. Domestic non-high-risk facilities are to be inspected not less than once in the seven-year period after enactment, and not less than once every five years thereafter.
Food safety plans	Requires all establishments to prepare and have preapproved "HACCP" (hazard analysis and critical control point) plans determining risks, controlling them (with documentation)	Prior to FSMA, facilities followed general regulations on good manufacturing practices (GMPs) to address safe handling and plant sanitation—except a form of HACCP required for seafood, low-acid canned foods, juices. FSMA §103 created new requirements for facilities to evaluate hazards, implement preventive controls, monitor controls, and maintain records. FDA rulemaking is clarifying requirements under new written HACCP-type and/or broader written food safety plans as part of its so-called Hazard Analysis and Risk-Based Preventive Controls.

Activity	Food Safety and Inspection Service	Food and Drug Administration (Foods Program only)
Imports	Specified products only from countries where FSIS has determined "equivalence" of foreign safety system, with annual verification; imports exempt from prior notice but subject to reinspection at 150 import establishments (est. 10% reinspected)	Prior to FSMA, food safety system equivalence was not determined beforehand; reliance on inspections was at 300 ports (est. 1% of notified entries inspected). FSMA provides for tighter controls and use certification or verification systems for imported foods (to be determined by FDA rulemaking). At least 600 foreign facilities must be inspected the year following enactment, and in each of the subsequent five years the number of foreign facilities inspected is to double.
Third party certification	Private labs accredited for chemical testing of meat and poultry (for imports, see above)	Prior to FSMA, there was no accreditation for food testing labs or use of third parties for import oversight. FSMA §202 requires FDA to establish a program for testing of food by accredited labs and to recognize accreditation bodies to accredit labs. FSMA §303 creates a system of accreditation of third-party auditors and audit agents to certify importing entities. FDA's rulemaking is ongoing.
On-farm oversight	FSIS inspection authority begins at slaughter plant	Prior to FSMA, those engaged solely in harvesting, storing or distributing raw agricultural commodities were generally exempt from registration, GMP regulations, and record-keeping. FSMA §105 created new farm-level requirements, particularly for fresh produce determined to be higher-risk (FDA rulemaking is ongoing). Some small farm businesses are exempt from regulation.
Labeling	Review and preapproval required for all labels	All foods must adhere to food labeling requirements such as statement of identity, declaration of net contents, nutrition labeling; labels cannot be false or misleading.
Notification Requirements	P.L. 110-246 §11017 amended meat and poultry laws to require an establishment to notify USDA if it has reason to believe that an adulterated or misbranded product has entered commerce	P.L. 110-85 (amended by FSMA) requires FDA to maintain a reportable food registry for industry to report food safety cases in order to help FDA better track patterns and target inspections. FSMA §204 provided for an enhanced tracing system for foods that FDA determines to pose a higher food safety risk. As part of the ongoing rulemaking process, FDA has launched product tracing pilots.
Recall Authority	No authority to mandate recalls; relies on voluntary efforts	Prior to FSMA, FDA had no authority to mandate recalls (except infant formula). FSMA §206 provides for mandatory recall authority where there is a reasonable probability that a food is adulterated or misbranded, and its use or exposure to it will cause serious adverse health consequences or death. Civil/criminal penalties apply for failure to comply with a recall order.

Source: Prepared by CRS.

Author Contact Information

Renée Johnson
Specialist in Agricultural Policy
rjohnson@crs.loc.gov, 7-9588

www.ingramcontent.com/pod-product-compliance
Lightning Source LLC
Chambersburg PA
CBHW081432310526
45790CB00020B/3736